Tales OF THE Unexpected

Stories told by **Jesus from Luke's Gospel**

Pete and Anne Woodcock

Jesus and you: Tales of the Unexpected
© Pete and Anne Woodcock/The Good Book Company 2009

This study guide is designed to be used with the Jesus and You: Tales of the Unexpected DVD also available from The Good Book Company. (DVD ISBN: 9781906334734)

Published by
The Good Book Company Ltd
Elm House, 37 Elm Road
New Malden, Surrey KT3 3HB, UK
Tel (UK): 0845 225 0880
Tel (Int): (+44) 208 942 0880
email: admin@thegoodbook.co.uk

Websites
UK: www.thegoodbook.co.uk
N America: www.thegoodbook.com
Australia: www.thegoodbook.com.au
New Zealand: www.thegoodbook.co.nz

Scripture quotations taken from the HOLY BIBLE, New International Reader's Version. Copyright © 1996, 1998 by International Bible Society. Used by permission of Hodder & Stoughton Publishers, a member of the Hodder Headline Group. All rights reserved.

ISBN: 9781906334727
Printed in India
Design by Steve Devane and André Parker

Contents

Welcome to Tales of the Unexpected 4

1 **The rich fool** 5
Luke 12 v 13-21

2 **The runaway son** 15
Luke 15 v 11-24

3 **The stay-at-home son** 25
Luke 15 v 11-32

4 **The Pharisee and the tax collector** 35
Luke 18 v 9-14

Welcome to Tales of the Unexpected

We hope that you will enjoy these four sessions. They will introduce you to Jesus Christ and his teaching.

In this booklet you will find a number of things to help you:

- Questions that you can talk about in your group
- Space to write down what you learn, if you want to
- The parts of the Bible that we will look at
- A summary of each DVD talk that we will watch
- Space to write down your own questions and comments

Tales of the Unexpected is for anyone and everyone who wants to find out about Jesus Christ. This means that...

- some of you know something about these stories of Jesus—but some of you don't know anything.
- some of you have been to church—but some of you are completely new to the Christian faith.
- some of you enjoy reading, writing and studying—but some of you haven't done this for years, and perhaps you never enjoyed it even then.
- some of you may be learning to speak English.

Whoever you are, don't worry—your group leader will help you and will explain everything you need to know.

So, time to get started and get into Tales of the Unexpected...

1 The rich fool
Luke 12 v 13-21

Think about a successful person.

- What things would show you that they were successful?

- Can you think of someone like this in a "soap" or other TV programme—or in the words of a song or rap?

The story

- Listen to the story Jesus told: Luke 12 v 16-21.
- You can read it for yourself on p12.

Optional Extra

Test yourself: how much can you remember?
Answer the questions in pairs, if you prefer.

- How many people are there in the story Jesus told?

- What is the man's job?

- What problem does he have?

- Who does he ask for advice?

- What does he decide to do about the problem?

- What is he looking forward to?

- What happens to him at the end of the story?

- What word does God use to describe him?

- At the end, Jesus says that this is how it will be for some people. What sort of people?

How well did you do?

Gatecrasher!

Listen to what was going on when Jesus told this story: Luke 12 v 13-16a.

You can read it for yourself on p12.

Think about it

1. What is the best description of the man in the crowd? Choose a, b or c.

    a   He wasn't interested in Jesus at all.

    b   He thought Jesus might be able to help him get some of the inheritance.

    c   He wanted to hear Jesus' teaching.

2. What did this man think would make his life really happy and successful? (Look at what Jesus said in v 15.)

3. Jesus wanted to show this man that he had a deeper problem than his family argument. Jesus shows us the man's real problem. What is it?

4. Popular songs, newspapers, magazines and TV shows often tell us how good it is to have loads of things.

    Can you think of any examples?

DOWNLOAD 1:1

(Summary on p13)

5. Which of these statements treat God in the same way that this man treated Jesus?

   a   "I pray every week that I will win the lottery."

   b   "Where was God when my house got flooded?"

   c   "Our Father in heaven, we pray that what you want will be done here on earth as it is in heaven."

6. How can we be like this man?

Ask yourself:

■ Imagine I can get Jesus' attention like this man. Is there something in my life that I want Jesus to sort out for me?

■ What sort of things do I pray for?

■ What stops me listening to the words of Jesus?

Me, myself and I

Listen to Jesus' story again: Luke 12 v 16-21.
You can read it for yourself on p12.

Think about it

1. How many times did the rich man say "me", "myself" or "I"?

- Who was he trying to please?

- Who did he turn to for advice (v 17)?

- Whose plan was he following?

- Who did he think was in control his life?

2. Who did he pray to?

3. What was the man's goal in life (see v 19)?

   Did he reach that goal?

4. How does Jesus show that this man was a fool?

DOWNLOAD 1:2
(Summary on p13)

5. "Most of the time, ordinary people live as if there is no God. Even if people say that they believe in God, they don't live as if he is real."

What shows us that this is true?

6. How do people build "bigger storerooms" in their lives?

7. Why do people fail to prepare for death?

Ask yourself:

- If the story stopped at the end of verse 19, would I like to be this man?
- If I were to die tonight, what would Jesus say about my life?

Really rich!

DOWNLOAD 1:3

(Summary on p13)

The big question: Where am I in this story?

- Am I in verse 13?—just wanting Jesus to help me with my own plans.
- Am I in verses 16-18?—everything is going well for me, and I'm making plans just for this life.
- Have I come to verse 20?—I see that all these plans are foolish, and will mean nothing to me when my life is taken from me.

"For you know the grace of our Lord Jesus Christ, that though he was rich, yet for your sakes he became poor, so that you through his poverty might become rich."

2 Corinthians 8 v 9 (The Bible: New International Version)

My questions and comments

1 Bible text

The rich fool
Luke 12 v 13-21

13 Someone in the crowd spoke to Jesus. "Teacher," he said, "tell my brother to divide the family property with me."

14 Jesus replied, "Friend, who made me a judge or umpire between you?"

15 Then he said to them, "Watch out! Be on your guard against wanting to have more and more things. Life is not made up of how much a person has."

16 Then Jesus told them a story. He said, "A certain rich man's land produced a good crop.

17 "He thought to himself, 'What should I do? I don't have any place to store my crops.'

18 "Then he said, 'This is what I'll do. I will tear down my storerooms and build bigger ones. I will store all my grain and my other things in them.

19 'I'll say to myself, "You have plenty of good things stored away for many years. Take life easy. Eat, drink and have a good time."'

20 "But God said to him, 'You foolish man! This very night I will take your life away from you. Then who will get what you have prepared for yourself?'

21 "That is how it will be for anyone who stores things away for himself but is not rich in God's eyes."

Downloads

Here is a summary of each Download to help you remember what was said.

DOWNLOAD 1:1

- Jesus is the world's greatest teacher. In Luke chapter 12 he has been talking about some of the most important subjects ever.
- When the man in the crowd interrupts Jesus, he shows he is not interested in what Jesus thinks is important. He is only interested in what he thinks is important.
- This man thinks getting his share of money from his brother is the most important thing.
- This man is interested in being rich with money. He is not interested in being rich towards God.
- Jesus tells us to beware of greed. In his story he will show that you can be rich in this world, and yet be completely poor towards God.

DOWNLOAD 1:2

- The rich farmer in the story looks very successful, until you get to verse 20.
- Jesus shows that the rich farmer was a complete failure because he made three big mistakes.
- Mistake 1: He lived as if there is no God.
- Mistake 2: He lived as if this world is all there is.
- Mistake 3: He lived as if there is no Judgment Day.

DOWNLOAD 1:3

- Jesus wants us to ask ourselves: "Am I rich in God's eyes?" "Am I rich in the way God wants?" and "How can I be rich toward God?"
- Only Jesus Christ can make us rich in God's eyes.
- The way to be rich towards God begins with listening to Jesus.

2 The runaway son
Luke 15 v 11-24

Summary so far:

■ We are only truly rich if we are rich in God's eyes (rich in the way God wants).

Think about freedom.

■ What does it mean to be free?
And how do you know if you are not free?

■ Can you think of any songs or films that show freedom?

The story

■ Listen to the first part of the story: Luke 15 v 11-24.
■ You can read it for yourself on p21-22.

Optional Extra

Test yourself: how much can you remember?
Fill in the gaps in pairs, if you prefer.

There was a man who had two sons. The younger son asked his father for his share of the (1)_____, so the father divided it between his sons. The younger son got all his things together and set off for (2)_____. There he wasted all his money in (3)_____ living. After he had spent everything, there came a time when there was no (4)_____ anywhere, and he was poor and hungry. So he got a job (5)_____. He was so hungry that he wanted to eat the (6)_____, but no one gave him anything. ▶

When he came to his senses, he said to himself: "All my father's (7)_____ have plenty of food. But I am here, almost dying with hunger. I will go back to my father and say: 'Father, I have (8)_____ against God and against you. I am no longer fit to be called (9)____ _____.'" But while the son was still a long way off, the father saw him and was sorry for him. The father ran to his son, (10)_____ him and (11)_____ him.

The son began to tell his father what he had planned to say. But the father said to his servant: "Quick! Bring the (12)_____ and put it on him. Put a (13)_____ on his finger and (14)_____ on his feet. Get the (15)_____ and kill it so we can have a big dinner and celebrate. My son was dead, but now he is alive again! He was lost, but now he is found!" So they began to celebrate.

How well did you do?

Gimme gimme!

Listen again to the beginning of the story: Luke 15 v 11-13.
You can read it for yourself on p21.

Think about it

1. When does a son or daughter normally get the family property from their parents?

   ■ The younger son wanted his share of the family property "now". By asking this, what was he really saying to his father?

2. What did the younger son do when he got his money?

■ What does this show about his attitude to his father?

3. What did this father do?

DOWNLOAD 2:1

(Summary on p23)

4. Think of some ways in which people today treat God and his gifts in the same way that the younger son treated his father.

Ask yourself:

■ How do I treat God in the same way that the younger son treated his father?

Wasted!

Listen again to the next part of the story: Luke 15 v 14-19.
You can read it for yourself on p21-22.

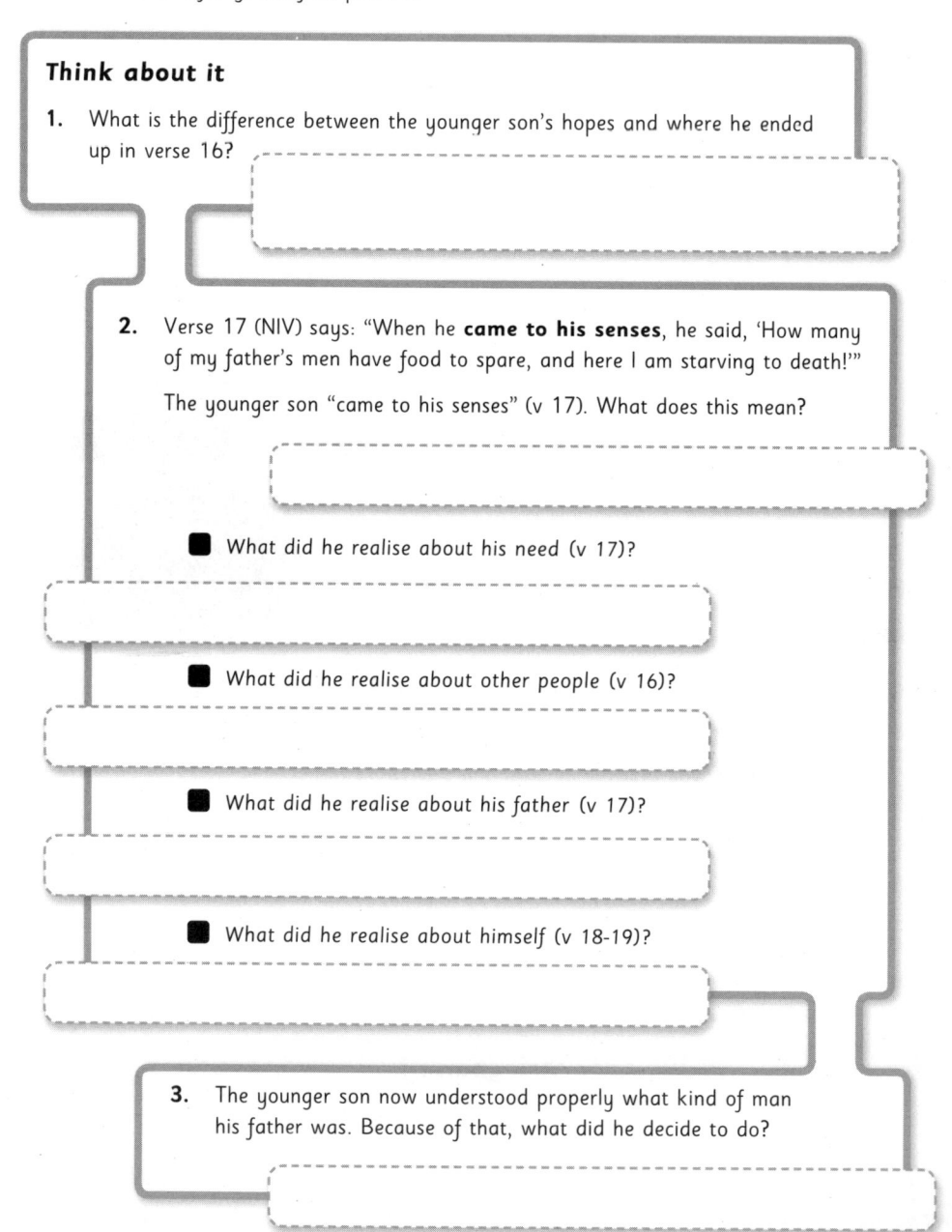

Think about it

1. What is the difference between the younger son's hopes and where he ended up in verse 16?

2. Verse 17 (NIV) says: "When he **came to his senses**, he said, 'How many of my father's men have food to spare, and here I am starving to death!'"

   The younger son "came to his senses" (v 17). What does this mean?

   ■ What did he realise about his need (v 17)?

   ■ What did he realise about other people (v 16)?

   ■ What did he realise about his father (v 17)?

   ■ What did he realise about himself (v 18-19)?

3. The younger son now understood properly what kind of man his father was. Because of that, what did he decide to do?

DOWNLOAD 2:2

(Summary on p23)

4. Jesus wants us to come to our senses. What will it mean for us to do this? What must we realise about...

- our need?

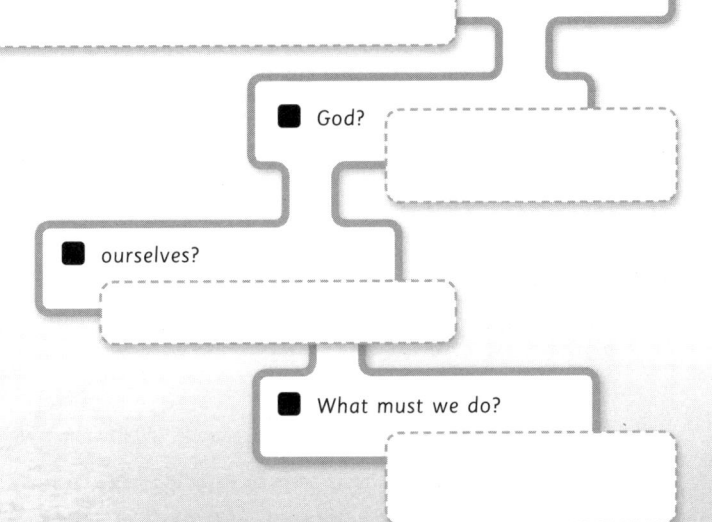

- God?

- ourselves?

- What must we do?

Ask yourself:

- Have I come to my senses, like the younger son?
- Like the younger son, have I ever admitted that I have sinned against God, and I am not worthy to be his child?

Homecoming!

Listen again to the last part of the story: Luke 15 v 20-24.
You can read it for yourself on p22.

Think about it

1. What did the father do when his son came home? List all the things that he did (v 20-24).

2. Which of these do you find most surprising? Why?

DOWNLOAD 2:3

(Summary on p23)

The big question: Where am I in this story?

- Am I in verse 12?—wanting to take God's gifts but not wanting God.

- Am I in verse 13?—things seem to be going quite well and I'm living how I want to live.

- Am I in verses 14-16?—I feel as if I have spent everything and I'm now on my own.

- Am I in verse 17?—I'm coming to my senses and beginning to realise that I have made a great mistake in leaving God out of my life.

- Am I in verse 20?—where I know I have come back to God and I understand something of his love for me.

"To all who received [Jesus Christ], to those who believed in his name, he gave the right to become children of God."

John 1 v 12 (The Bible: New International Version)

My questions and comments

2 Bible text

The runaway son
Luke 15 v 11-24

11   Jesus continued, "There was a man who had two sons.

12   "The younger son spoke to his father. He said, 'Father, give me my share of the family property.' So the father divided his property between his two sons.

13   "Not long after that, the younger son packed up all he had. Then he left for a country far away. There he wasted his money on wild living.

14   "He spent everything he had. Then the whole country ran low on food. So the son didn't have what he needed.

15   "He went to work for someone who lived in that country, who sent him to the fields to feed the pigs.

16   "The son wanted to fill his stomach with the food the pigs were eating. But no one gave him anything.

17 "Then he began to think clearly again [or – he came to his senses]. He said, 'How many of my father's hired workers have more than enough food! But here I am dying from hunger!

18 'I will get up and go back to my father. I will say to him, "Father, I have sinned against heaven. And I have sinned against you.

19 "I am no longer fit to be called your son. Make me like one of your hired workers."'

20 "So he got up and went to his father. While the son was still a long way off, his father saw him. He was filled with tender love [or – compassion] for his son. He ran to him. He threw his arms around him and kissed him.

21 "The son said to him, 'Father, I have sinned against heaven and against you. I am no longer fit to be called your son.'

22 "But the father said to his servants, 'Quick! Bring the best robe and put it on him. Put a ring on his finger and sandals on his feet.

23 'Bring the fattest calf and kill it. Let's have a big dinner and celebrate.

24 'This son of mine was dead. And now he is alive again. He was lost. And now he is found.' So they began to celebrate."

Downloads

Here is a summary of each Download to help you remember what was said.

DOWNLOAD 2:1

- Jesus' story of the runaway son is not about how to treat our parents, but about how we treat God and how God treats us.
- The father represents God, and the two sons show different ways in which people like us turn away from God.
- By demanding his share of the family property, the younger son was really saying that he wished his father was dead!
- The younger son left his father because he was certain that he could run his life better on his own.
- Like the younger son, we take the good things that God has given us and then run our life on our own, as if God is dead.

DOWNLOAD 2:2

- At first, the younger son had a good time. But when his money ran out no one helped him.
- He thought he could make a home for himself away from the father, but he ended up feeding pigs and starving.
- Even if we have all that this world can give us, we won't find true satisfaction or freedom. "The party is always followed by the morning after."
- The younger son came to his senses when he realised that he needed to go home to his father.
- He knew he had sinned against his father. But he also knew how good his father was. So he had hope that he would be accepted back.

DOWNLOAD 2:3

- His father was waiting for him. He ran to him, and hugged and kissed him in his dirty pig-feeding clothes.
- The father enjoyed having his son home again and celebrated with a great party.
- Despite all the things in our lives that make us unclean, God wants to welcome us back into his family.
- God has "run to us" by sending Jesus. In Jesus, our "dirty clothes" are removed and we are given "new clothes"—we are forgiven and accepted back into God's family.
- Where are you in this story?

3 The stay-at-home son
Luke 15 v 11-32

Summary so far:

- We are only truly rich if we are rich in God's eyes.
- We need to come to our senses. We need to realise God is a generous father who will welcome us back.

Think about fairness.

- "It's not fair!" Where do you hear that? And what does it show about human nature?

The story

Last session we looked at the first half of Jesus' story about two sons.

- Now listen to the whole story: Luke 15 v 11-32.
- You can read it for yourself on p31-32.

Optional Extra

Test yourself: how much can you remember?
Answer the true or false questions in pairs, if you prefer.

a. The father gave some property to both of his sons. **T / F**
b. The younger son left home because he wanted to look after pigs. **T / F**
c. The younger son left home because he couldn't get on with his father. **T / F**
d. To start with, the younger son didn't care about his relationship with his father. **T / F**
e. The younger son came home again because he wanted more money. **T / F**
f. The older son felt sorry for his brother. **T / F**
g. The older son enjoyed working for his father. **T / F**
h. The older son was angry with his father as well as with his brother. **T / F**
i. The father loved both his sons. **T / F**
j. At the end, the older son made up with his father. **T / F**

Who's a good boy then?

Listen again to the second part of the story: Luke 15 v 25-32.
You can read it for yourself on p32.

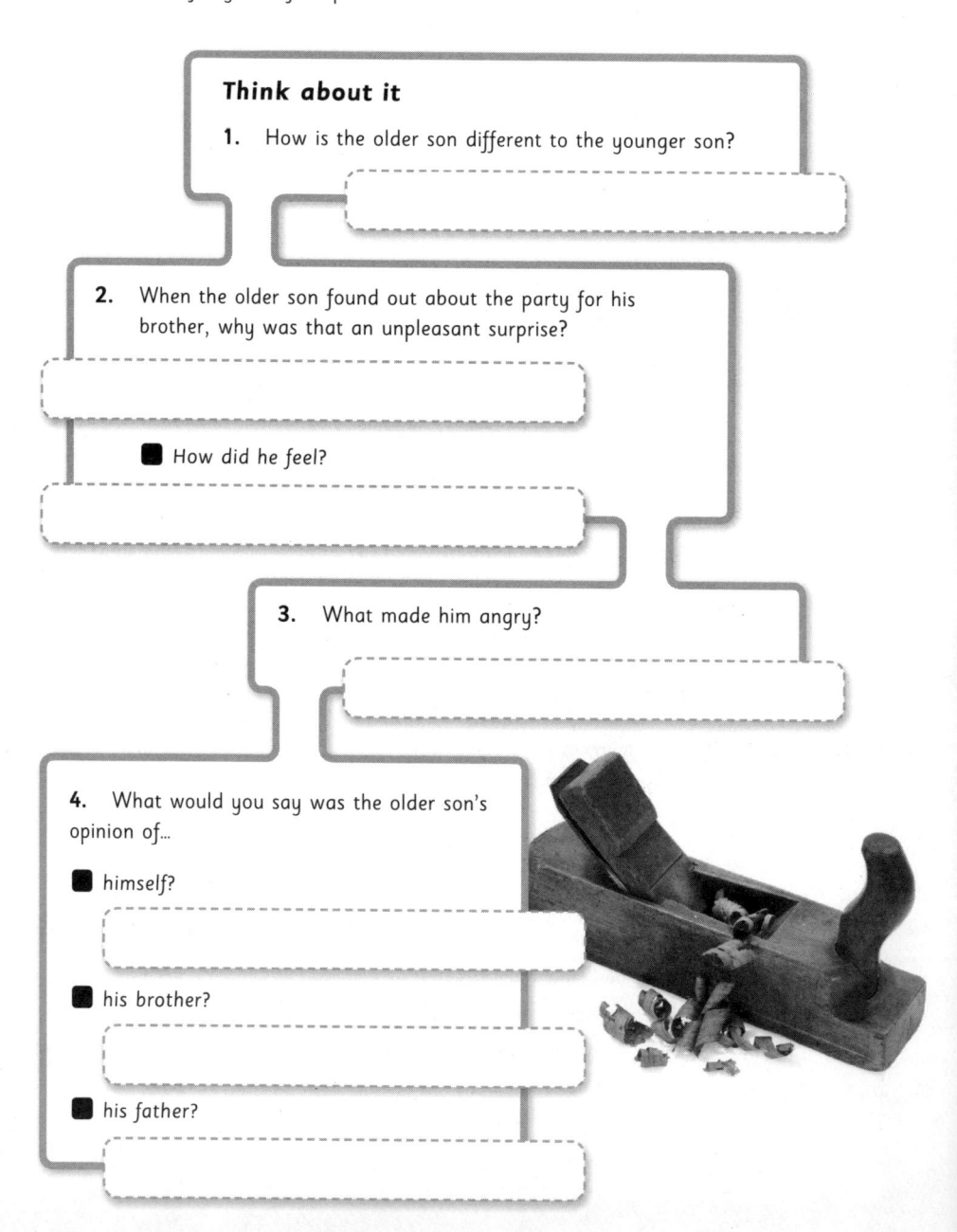

Think about it

1. How is the older son different to the younger son?

2. When the older son found out about the party for his brother, why was that an unpleasant surprise?

   ■ How did he feel?

3. What made him angry?

4. What would you say was the older son's opinion of...

   ■ himself?

   ■ his brother?

   ■ his father?

DOWNLOAD 3:1

(Summary on p34)

5. In truth, how good was the older son? (Did he do what his father wanted at the end of the story?)

6. What did he really think of his father? Look at verses 29-30.

7. How like his father was the older son? (How much did he share what his father loved and longed for?)

8. What did he really want from his father?

Ask yourself:

■ Have I ever treated God like a machine that sells chocolate bars?

Same difference

Listen again to the end of the story: Luke 15 v 31-32.
You can read it for yourself on p32.

Think about it

1. How similar are the two brothers? (Look at the next questions to help you answer this.)

At the beginning of the story...

■ what did the younger son want?

■ what did he not want?

At the end of the story...

■ what does the older son want?

■ what does he not want?

DOWNLOAD 3:2

(Summary on p34)

2. Look at what the father says to the older son in verse 31.
What does the father think is the most important thing in their relationship?

■ Does the younger son now have this kind of relationship with his father? (Where is the younger son at the end of the story?)

■ Does the older son now have this kind of relationship with his father? (Where is the older son at the end of the story?)

3. How does the story show us that God is very different from what we often expect?

Ask yourself:

■ Which son am I most like?

Relationship

DOWNLOAD 3:3

(Summary on p34)

The big question: Where am I in this story?

- Am I in verse 28?—I'm angry that God welcomes "younger sons".
- Am I in verse 29?—treating God as a slave-master, rather than my loving Father.
- Am I in verses 29-30?—I can see loads of people that I am better than.
- Am I in verse 28?—I'm outside the party and I know nothing of God's forgiveness and celebration.

> "Many will say to me on that day, 'Lord, Lord, did we not prophesy in your name, and in your name drive out demons and perform many miracles?' Then I will tell them plainly, 'I never knew you.'"
>
> Matthew 7 v 22-23 (The Bible: New International Version)

My questions and comments

3 Bible text

The stay-at-home son
Luke 15 v 11-32

11 Jesus continued, "There was a man who had two sons.

12 "The younger son spoke to his father. He said, 'Father, give me my share of the family property.' So the father divided his property between his two sons.

13 "Not long after that, the younger son packed up all he had. Then he left for a country far away. There he wasted his money on wild living.

14 "He spent everything he had. Then the whole country ran low on food. So the son didn't have what he needed.

15 "He went to work for someone who lived in that country, who sent him to the fields to feed the pigs.

16 "The son wanted to fill his stomach with the food the pigs were eating. But no one gave him anything.

17 "Then he began to think clearly again [or – he came to his senses]. He said, 'How many of my father's hired workers have more than enough food! But here I am dying from hunger!

18 'I will get up and go back to my father. I will say to him, "Father, I have sinned against heaven. And I have sinned against you.

19 "I am no longer fit to be called your son. Make me like one of your hired workers."'

20 "So he got up and went to his father. While the son was still a long way off, his father saw him. He was filled with tender love [or – compassion] for his son. He ran to him. He threw his arms around him and kissed him.

21 "The son said to him, 'Father, I have sinned against heaven and against you. I am no longer fit to be called your son.'

22 "But the father said to his servants, 'Quick! Bring the best robe and put it on him. Put a ring on his finger and sandals on his feet.

23 'Bring the fattest calf and kill it. Let's have a big dinner and celebrate.

24 'This son of mine was dead. And now he is alive again. He was lost. And now he is found.' So they began to celebrate."

25 "The older son was in the field. When he came near the house, he heard music and dancing.

26 "So he called one of the servants. He asked him what was going on.

27 'Your brother has come home,' the servant replied. 'Your father has killed the fattest calf. He has done this because your brother is back safe and sound.'

28 "The older brother became angry. He refused to go in. So his father went out and begged him.

29 "But he answered his father, 'Look! All these years I've worked like a slave for you. I have always obeyed your orders. You never gave me even a young goat so I could celebrate with my friends.

30 'But this son of yours wasted your money with some prostitutes. Now he comes home. And for him you kill the fattest calf!'

31 'My son,' the father said, 'you are always with me. Everything I have is yours.

32 'But we had to celebrate and be glad. This brother of yours was dead. And now he is alive again. He was lost. And now he is found.'"

Bible text mentioned in Download 3:1

Luke 15 v 1-10

1. The tax collectors and "sinners" were all gathering around to hear Jesus.

2. But the Pharisees and the teachers of the law were whispering among themselves. They said, "This man welcomes sinners and eats with them."

3. Then Jesus told them a story.

4. He said, "Suppose one of you has 100 sheep and loses one of them. Won't he leave the 99 in the open country? Won't he go and look for the one lost sheep until he finds it?

5. "When he finds it, he will joyfully put it on his shoulders

6. and go home. Then he will call his friends and neighbours together. He will say, 'Be joyful with me. I have found my lost sheep.'

7. "I tell you, it will be the same in heaven. There will be great joy when one sinner turns away from sin. Yes, there will be more joy than for 99 godly people who do not need to turn away from their sins.

8. "Or suppose a woman has ten silver coins and loses one. She will light a lamp and sweep the house. She will search carefully until she finds the coin.

9. "And when she finds it, she will call her friends and neighbours together. She will say, 'Be joyful with me. I have found my lost coin.'

10. "I tell you, it is the same in heaven. There is joy in heaven over one sinner who turns away from sin."

Downloads

Here is a summary of each Download to help you remember what was said.

DOWNLOAD 3:1

- The main point of Jesus' story about the two sons is to get us to think about the older son.
- This story is the last of three stories told by Jesus in Luke chapter 15. Each one is about something that is lost—in a place where it ought not to be. In each story someone goes to look for the thing that is lost.
- At the end of the story of the two sons, the older son is as lost as the younger son was. He is not where he ought to be—in the party, with the father.
- The older son looks good, but inside he is angry with his father because he thinks he has no reward for his hard work. He treats his father like a machine that sells chocolate bars.
- We treat God like a chocolate bar machine—we think that if we do good things, God should reward us. Just as no one wants a relationship with a machine, so we don't really want to know God as our Father.
- It is possible to be a hard-working, clean-living, decent, religious person but still be lost, because we are miles away from the heart of God.

DOWNLOAD 3:2

- The people who find this teaching of Jesus most difficult are those who are very good and religious. They are "older son" people and there are four things that we can learn about them from Jesus' story.
    1. "Older son" people live good and religious lives because they are pleasing themselves, not because they love God and enjoy pleasing him.
    2. "Older son" people compare themselves with others who are worse than them.
    3. "Older son" people can't bear the idea that someone, however bad, can call God "Father", without having to do good stuff first.
    4. "Older son" people are more lost than "younger son" people. That's because they don't know that they are lost.

DOWNLOAD 3:3

- Jesus teaches that what is most important is not what we do for God, but what relationship we have with him.
- The story of the stay-at-home son teaches us that good people too need to come to their senses and seek a true relationship with God.
- Where are you in this story?

4 The Pharisee and the tax collector
Luke 18 v 9-14

Summary so far:

- We are only truly rich if we are rich in God's eyes.
- We need to come to our senses. We need to realise God is a generous father who will welcome us back.
- Being a good person means nothing if we don't know God as our loving Father.

Imagine...

Imagine a religious suicide-bomber... blowing himself and other people around him to pieces. Imagine that one second later that suicide-bomber is standing before God.

- What does he expect from God?

- What do you think he will discover?

The story

- Listen to the whole story: Luke 18 v 9-14.
- You can read it for yourself on p42.

Optional Extra

Test yourself: how much can you remember? Choose the correct answers in pairs, if you prefer.

A. Jesus told this story to people who...

  a. were right with God.
  b. thought they were right with God.
  c. thought everyone was right with God.

B. a. Both the Pharisee and the tax collector went to the temple to pray.
    b. Only the Pharisee went to the temple to pray.
    c. The Pharisee went to the temple to pray and the tax collector went to collect taxes.

C. a. The Pharisee prayed with the tax collector.
    b. The Pharisee helped the tax collector to pray.
    c. The Pharisee prayed by himself.

D. a. The Pharisee felt good about himself.
    b. The Pharisee felt bad about himself.
    c. The Pharisee wasn't sure what he thought about himself.

E. a. The tax collector didn't know what to say to God.
    b. The tax collector put his trust in God's kindness.
    c. The tax collector was too afraid to speak to God.

F. According to Jesus…

    a. God forgives those who admit they have done wrong and who ask him for help.
    b. God forgives everyone.
    c. God forgives people who are confident about their goodness.

How well did you do?

A shocking end!

Listen to the whole story again: Luke 18 v 9-14.
You can read it for yourself on p42.

Think about it

1. Who was Jesus teaching when he told this story (v 9)?

2. Look at the end of the story in v 14. Who was right with God?

Who was not right with God?

3. What is good about the Pharisee's life (v 11-12)?

4. Look at the Pharisee's prayer.

How many times does he mention God?

How many times does he mention himself?

Why does he think he is right with God?

5. The Pharisee compares himself with the tax collector. What does he think of the tax collector?

DOWNLOAD 4:1

(Summary on p43)

6. Today, what kind of people do you think are right with God?

■ What kind of people do you think cannot be right with God?

Ask yourself:

■ How much like the Pharisee am I?

A wonderful end!

Think about it

1. How did these two men stand when they prayed? How were they different?

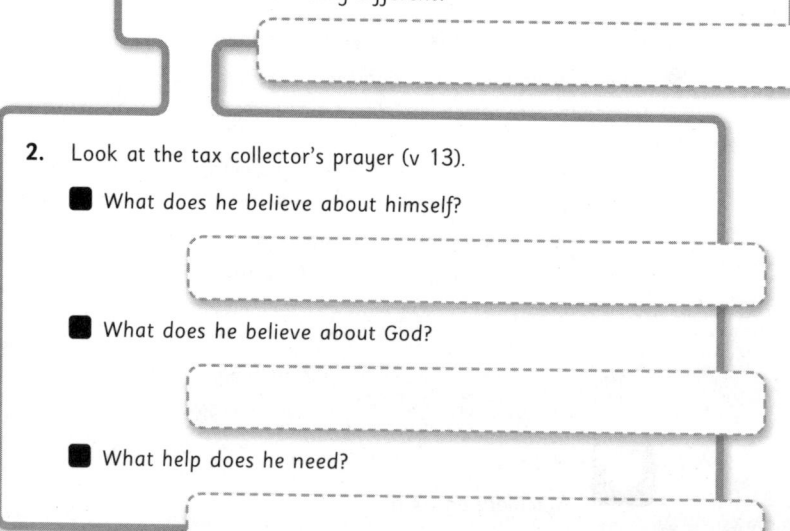

2. Look at the tax collector's prayer (v 13).

■ What does he believe about himself?

■ What does he believe about God?

■ What help does he need?

3. We've seen that the Pharisee is trusting in himself. What do you think the tax collector is trusting in?

DOWNLOAD 4:2

(Summary on p43)

4. Look at verse 14. What does Jesus want us to learn from this story?

■ In what way was the tax collector humble (brought down)?

■ In what way did the Pharisee lift himself up?

5. How are people who trust God's mercy different from people who try to be good enough for God?

6. Why do you think so many people, like the Pharisee, ignore God's mercy?

Ask yourself:

■ What stops you from being like the tax collector?

Mercy for you

DOWNLOAD 4:3

(Summary on p43)

The big question: Where am I in the chart?

Who?	Not right with God	Why?	Right with God	Why?
The rich fool	✗	Not rich before God. Never thinks about him.		
The younger son	✗	Walks away. Wants to run his own life.	✓	Comes to his senses. Turns back.
The older son	✗	Outside the party. Thinks he is good enough.		
The Pharisee	✗	Thinks he is religious enough.		
The tax collector	✗	A sinner.	✓	Confesses his sin. Trusts in God's mercy.
Me				

"God demonstrates his own love for us in this: While we were still sinners, Christ died for us."

Romans 5 v 8 (The Bible: New International Version)

My questions and comments

4 Bible text

The Pharisee and the tax collector
Luke 18 v 9-14

9 Jesus told a story to some people who were sure they were right with God. They looked down on everybody else.

10 He said to them, "Two men went up to the temple to pray. One was a Pharisee. The other was a tax collector.

11 "The Pharisee stood up and prayed about himself. 'God, I thank you that I am not like other people,' he said. 'I am not like robbers or those who do other evil things. I am not like those who commit adultery. I am not even like this tax collector.

12 'I fast twice a week. And I give a tenth of all I get.'

13 "But the tax collector stood not very far away. He would not even look up to heaven. He beat his chest and said, 'God, have mercy on me. I am a sinner.'

14 "I tell you, the tax collector went home accepted by God. But not the Pharisee. Everyone who lifts himself up will be brought down. And anyone who is brought down will be lifted up."

Downloads

Here is a summary of each Download to help you remember what was said.

DOWNLOAD 4:1

- Jesus puts two people into this story who are completely different. One tries to be very good—the Pharisee, who keeps laws very strictly and believes he is one of God's special people. The other is very bad—a tax collector, which means he is a traitor and a thief.
- Jesus turns everything upside down. He tells us that the tax collector went home right with God, but the Pharisee did not.
- The real difference between the two men is who or what they are trusting in as they come to God.
- The Pharisee trusts in himself. He prays about himself and he believes that he is ok.

DOWNLOAD 4:2

- The tax collector knows that he is guilty of sin, and he knows that God knows. The first step to be right with God is to know that you are not right with him.
- The tax collector knows that only God can help him and so he asks God to have mercy on him.
- The tax collector asks God to be "mercy-seated" to him. What happened at the mercy seat in the temple shows us how God forgives sinful people—a perfect substitute is punished instead of sinners.
- Jesus is the Lamb of God who takes away the sins of the world. He was perfect, but when he died, he was treated like a sinner.
- The next steps to being right with God are to ask God for mercy and then to trust in what God has done for us—sending Jesus to die on the cross.

DOWNLOAD 4:3

- Some people find out the truth—that although they think they are right with God, they are not—but they won't listen to the truth. This is because they don't want to make themselves humble.
- But the truth about Jesus can only help us if we make ourselves humble—if we are like the younger son and the tax collector, not like the rich farmer, the older son or the Pharisee.
- God, in his kindness, has spoken to us through all of these stories of Jesus—so that we might come to our senses and say: "God, be mercy-seated to me, a sinner".

Notes and comments:

Notes and comments:

Notes and comments:

Notes and comments:

Notes and comments: